A BOUQUET OF POEMS

A COLLECTION OF 25 POEMS

UMESH C BHATT

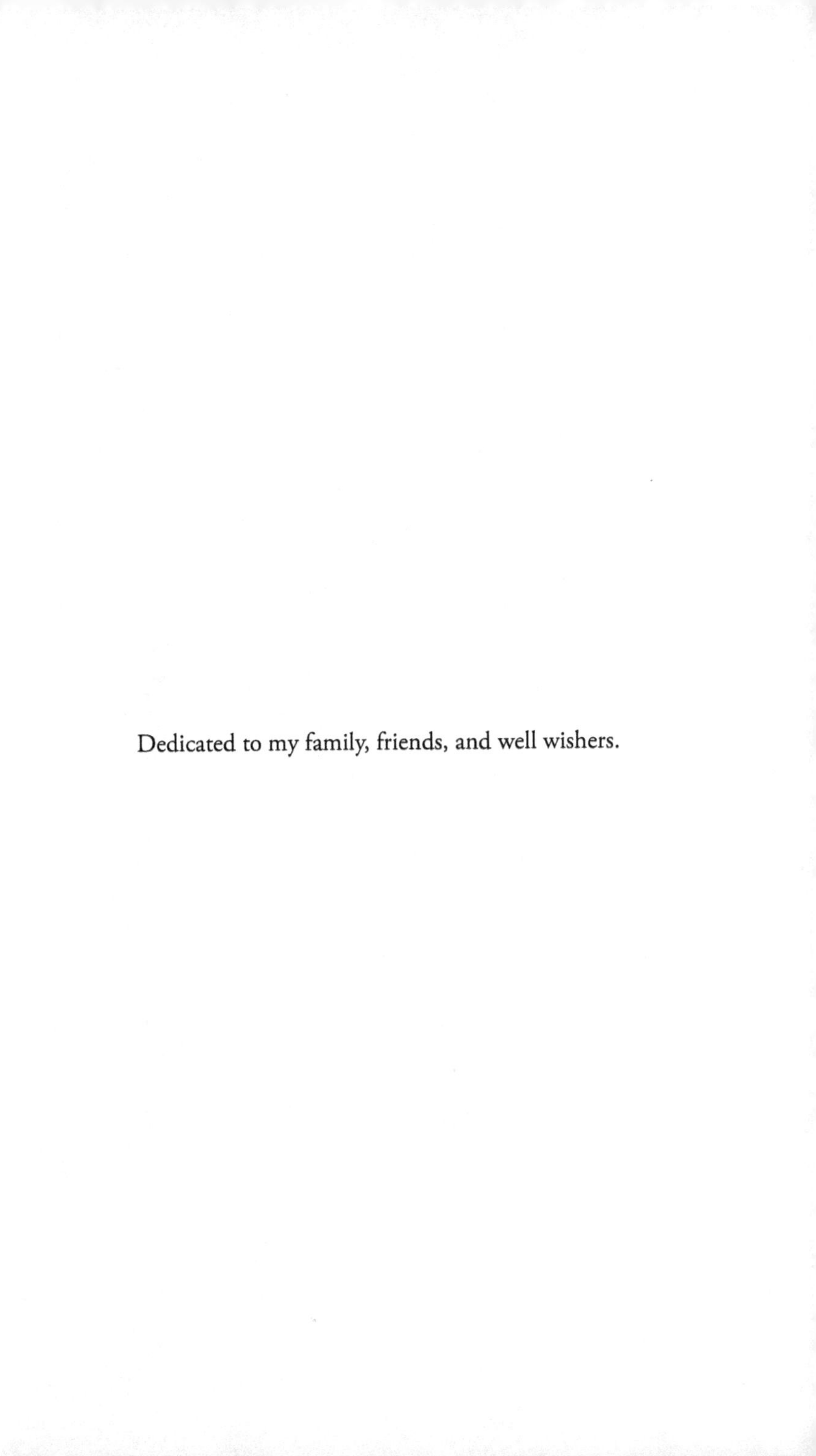

Dedicated to my family, friends, and well wishers.

Contents

Contents

Foreword

Poems are a great way to depict the human emotions and sentiments. We all experience a variety of situations and circumstances in our lives affecting us in different ways and acoordingly our thought process and mindsets manifest itself. External stimuli affect our minds and feelings in a big way.

Poetry is an effective medium of presenting subtle human feelings and emotions in black and white. In this collection of poems I have tried to cover various topics like love, fear, separation, shadows, ambitons, and many more and I hope readers would like and enjoy these creative compilations.

1. My Shadow Remains With Me

"The brighter the light, the darker the shadow."
-- Carl Jung

The word shadow is not only mysterious but also baffling sometimes as some of us are always having its presence felt very near to us, even in absence of light, and we cannot get rid of it by any possible means in this world.

Shadow generally connotates a dark and sad undercurrent under it and is understood as a matter related to negative territories. So, presence of shadow in any form is a negative attribute and can create misery and bad times in one's life.

I am not only talking about physical shadow which we usually find in a lighted place but it could be anything which happened in past as a bad or unpleasant memory or a criminal act by someone or something which happened but cannot be erased from our memories because we were instrumental or involved in doing that unpleasant action.

From that perspective this poem is an effort to showcase whether one can get rid of one's shadow defined in a different way as above or is forced to live with it throughout one's life.

My shadow remains with me

My shadow is my companion,

It remains always with me.

Even if I do not want it,
It would not leave me free.
My shadow was born with me,
He is just like my twin.
It walks with me with same pace,
If I take a round, it also makes a spin.
One day I got an idea novel,
If I wish I could destroy my shadow.
It was simple and very ingenious,
Easier than moving my elbow.
The trick was really very simple,
I had to avoid Sun and light.
I would remain in shade and dark,
Shadow will have its own plight.
I started to do like that,
But a loud laughter followed me.
I am not there because of light,
In a snarling voice it told to me.
The shadow laughed and grinned at me,
Told me that it was my integral part.
It could not be destroyed by any means,
And it cannot be taken apart.
Now I feel it present there for good,
It is actually clung to me like a robe.
Would I ever get free from this shadow,
Now, I do not have any such hope.

2. A Feeling of Sonder

"It's a strange feeling, realising that other people you don't know have their own, full lives that don't touch yours."
-- Mackenzi Lee

There are some uncommon words or rather rare words or words that many people do not know and do not use them. Even if we know the meaning it is indeed very difficult to use them because we had not used them in the past. Some of these words are so obscure that we have to search for them in the dictionary or other reference places to know their exact meaning as then only it is possible to use them in our creative writings.

I remember when I was doing my graduation then one of my friends asked me if I knew a word spelt like 'honouraficabilitudinity'. I simply told that I didn't know about it. Was it there in the dictionary? I was told that yes it was in one of the editions of the Oxford dictionary.

In my curiosity, I asked what did the word mean. I was told that it simply meant honour! So, the lesson I learnt was that sometimes the uncommon or obscure words might not be very different in meaning from the available words and that could be one reason why people are not using them.

There is a very unique but uncommon and unusual word 'sonder' which incidentally I heard for the first time and while going through its meaning in various sources came to know that it precisely means - 'the realization that each random passerby is living a life as vivid and complex as your own - populated with their own ambitions, friends, routines, worries and inherited craziness'.

After going through that small literally exercise, I have now tried to use this word in my following poem to depict the story of a person who thought he was the only one born miserable on this earth while the fact was that there were many like him and many more were more miserable than him. Once he comes to know this fact then he becomes a normal person and starts struggling in his life as most of us routinely do.

A feeling of sonder

I always thought that,

I was the unfortunate one.

While everyone else enjoying life,

I was the unfavoured son.

There are people who talk pleasantly,

with friends and strangers.

But when I talk to them,

They simply show me their cold shoulders.

I felt myself the most unhappy,

And the sad person on this earth.

I was not getting any success anywhere,

And found me of no worth.

My life became a pitiable thing,

It made me frail and fragile.
My sleep was disturbed much,
My efforts were all futile.
I started taking walks in the dark nights,
Not knowing what else to do.
And then it happened,
when I encountered this ghostly hoodoo.
He was looking very sad,
And each of his eyes had one big tear.
I felt sympathetic to him,
I talked to him without any fear.
He told me that once he was very powerful,
But destiny had something else in mind.
His master was unhappy with him,
Then he was punished and fined.
I know everything I can see everything,
I know about you all dear.
But I can't do anything and am a shadow only,
You would not realise my fear.

He finished narrating about his plight,
But my mind was agog with thoughts.
Even a ghost could be so helpless,
Then what about the earthly noughts.

I realised that I was not the,
Only person suffering on Earth.

I got a feeling of sonder,
And revitalized my worth.

• 6 •

3. Anxiety Chasing Me to Grave

"Worrying is carrying tomorrow's load with today's strength-carrying two days at once. It is moving into tomorrow ahead of time. Worrying doesn't empty tomorrow of its sorrow, it empties today of its strength."

-- Corrie Ten Boom

Anxiety is a natural feeling in our lives. It is very rare if a person doesn't possess it. Most of the people on this earth are affected by anxiety in one way or another. It is said that a minimum level of anxiety is very necessary for our progress and development. This is the amount of anxiety that forces us to work hard in our lives and continuously tread ahead in our careers. At the same time, a large amount of anxiety would be harmful to us affecting our mental as well as physical health.

It will be a good thing to accept some amount of anxiety in our lives as a way of life and adjust to it in such a manner that it can be used in a positive and constructive way in our lives rather than to curse it for umpteen number of times without getting rid of it.

As said, a high amount of anxiety in our lives is not a good thing as it will affect our mental and physical health significantly and we should be very careful and cautious on that front to avoid it at any cost. Experts and consultants suggest many ways to fight this enemy known as anxiety but ultimately it is the individual who has to find ways to control and eradicate this evil from one's life. It will not leave us and we have to keep it away or at the minimum threshold.

Anxiety chasing me to grave

My anxiety was born with me,
I did not know that at that time.
Then while growing up, I came to know about it,
And accepted it as a usual sign.
During my school days,
I always worried for my exams.
Anxiety time to time gripped me,
I had insomnia and occasional spasms.
My health was affected,
But I had scored good marks.
I was happy to get admission in college,
Thinking of career sparks.
College study was more challenging,
And my anxiety levels increased.
Competitions were getting stiffer,
All my excitements got ceased.
I was lucky to complete my course,
And also achieved a good score.
I felt happy and contented,
What else I wanted more.
Now the time came for getting a job,
And I was trying desperately for that.

Anxiety again enveloped me,
What if I am not able to secure a job.
Somehow I got a job of my liking,
I felt satisfied and as a warrior.
But it was only for a short time,
As I came to know about sustaining career.
Working and then rising in the career,
Required a series of fights.
Life seemed so difficult and challenging,
With anxiety crossing heights.
I am still working and working,
But anxiety remains there.
It would chase me to my grave,
And that is my only fear.

4. Dark Shadow of the Patience

I have conceived this poem based on the story of a girl who was patiently waiting for her boyfriend but he did not come back for her or could not come back due to some compelling reasons or was not in love with her contrary to her expectations and obviously, the poem depicting all this has a sad ending.

However, seeing to the positive side of it we can very well say that a person can even live under that shadow of waiting and patience exhibited by him or her in that matter or relationship. Waiting endlessly for anything is a test of patience but that does not mean that one has accepted defeat from one's destiny. Life can be carried forward even under that shadow. Waiting is not a negative thing in our lives. It is a sign of hope. Many people live in this world with hope only.

Failures and setbacks in relationships are common phenomenon that affects the individual also and many times could trigger depressive tendencies in them. The individual has to forget the past and come out of the old memories and chart a new path in one's life. Still, the shadow of old memories haunts people time and again and one has to manage that and overcome the depressive bouts.

Destiny sometimes tests our patience by playing challenging games with us but if we keep patience then we do not surrender to it so easily. That is the fight a bold and brave person has to put up in one's life and make the struggle of life meaningful.

Dark shadow of the patience

I was his childhood friend and we were studying in the same
class,
He was a tall and young boy and I was a girl wearing a
myopic glass.
He played so many sports and participated in tournaments,
While I fancied indoor games and other subtle
entertainments.
He was intelligent and good in his studies and talked less,
I was a mediocre girl in studies and talked more and was
careless.
We all went for camps and outings and played games on
holidays,
We were growing up and were going to theatre, movies and
plays.
I was fascinated with his ways, manners and behaviour,
He was so respectful so graceful and was my lovely dear.
He was friendly with everyone but gave me a special place,
I was able to read it in his eyes in those piercing blaze.
We grew up together and then chose our careers and went
our own ways,

He became an executive in a big company and I was
pursuing my computer craze.
I loved him but could not express my feelings and my
emotional bend,
I was simply waiting patiently for initiation from his end.
We were in constant touch and chatted regularly,
He always talked about his childhood days which were so
lovely.
I was patient enough and waiting for the signal of love from
him,
He chatted everything with me except showing his attraction
to me.
I could not understand whether he was testing me or testing
my patience,
But I had no other go except waiting for his expected future
presence.
Slowly our connections diminished and chats decreased,
Finally, they were limited only to the Christmas and New
year greets.
It was sad and brought a wind of sorrow with it rattling my
house fence,
I am still living in the dark shadow of the ambience of that
patience.

5. The Story of Sand Castle

"White sand, white foam, blue water - it's not a fantasy, it's real."

-- Marty Rubin

The word sand evokes myriads of thoughts in our minds and I was recollecting the time of my childhood when I learnt how to make a sandcastle on the beach. A child is very happy when its dreams are achieved in real life. But a child is oblivious of nature's cruelty and its occasional bizarre patterns of bringing distress and gloom. When the child grows into an adult he comes to know many of these things and also comes to know the relationship between our aspirations and results of our efforts. Anyway, that is the way people learn how to struggle in our lives and set our goals and objectives.

This poem is a culmination of similar thoughts coming into my mind and I am presenting it here. The end of the poem may look sad and pessimistic but that is the reality of our lives and we have to learn and face them to struggle in the journey ahead. Many time we can contemplate and plan in our lives for a happy and fruitful outcome of the actions but destiny has something else stored for us which could be a surprising and shocking thing in our lives.

The story of sand castle

That seashore was having,

A magnificent beach.

I was a child dwelling nearby,

And it was in my reach.

I was fascinated,

With the golden yellow sand.

It was lying there,

Spread under nature's hand.

I took it in my hands,

It was moist and cooling my fingertips.

I started moulding it,

And it took myriads of shapes and jibs.

I was excited to see it,

And use my creative outlet.

I was pondering if,

I could make a small castle set.

I sat down and started,

Converting my thoughts into shaping the sands.

Soon I was through with a castle,

Made entirely with my hands.

My dream was achieved,

As I fulfilled that long-cherished desire.

This was my creation,

Which could not be destroyed even with fire.

And then the inevitable happened,

Through the winds and their hassles deep.
A strong tide drenched me,
And the castle converted to a sand heap.

• 15 •

6. Riddle of Time

"Time flies over us, but leaves its shadow behind."
-- Nathaniel Hawthorne

Time is one of the most strange and peculiar dimensions in our lives. Science is yet to decipher the beginning of time and the probable end of time if at all that exists. There are many theories to explain the beginning of time and one of the most popular is the big bang event at time zero when this universe was supposed to be created but the obvious question asked by the common people is what was before the big bang event. So, explaining time is still an unsolved riddle and continues to remain like that till a logical answer is obtained supported by scientific explanation and data.

Scientific advancements have made it possible to observe the light or electromagnetic radiations coming from distant stars or heavenly bodies but what we are seeing today is the image of those bodies belonging to an earlier time and because of huge distances we cannot see them as they are today. What it simply means is that we are seeing them as they looked so many years (in fact millions of years) back.

With all those observations the mystery of time deepens further and we are forced to explain it based on some divine methodologies taking the help of factors like birth, death, and fate.

Riddle of time

Time is an elusive and strange entity,
Only flows in a forward direction.
We do not have any control on time,
It might be a divine and Godly action.
We are like a speck on the time line,
We perceive time only in small duration.
Our birth and death events are,
Only a matter of divine permission.
No one knows the extent of time line,
It stretches from deep past to distant future.
We all are small dots on that time line,
Whether a human being or any creature.
Time has no known beginning,
Neither has it an end discreet.
Events at different points in time,
Remain isolated and never meet.
Time is the essence of everything,
But nature of time is indeterminate.
Time is the ultimate reality,
And time is actually our fate.
Our lives are fixed intervals,
And every life ends with death.
But the entity time never dies,
And gloriously moves ahead.

7. Discovering Purpose of Life

"Work gives you meaning and purpose and life is empty without it."

-- Stephen Hawking

The word 'purpose' evokes many feelings in our minds and we should have some purpose identified in our lives failing which we would be like dead wood. But identifying the purpose correctly is not so easy and in its absence confusion and setbacks prevail.

Sometimes it becomes very difficult to identify our purpose because of a lack of understanding, confusion, and indecisiveness which are so common and inherent in many of us. So, we might make efforts in work that do not match the direction of our purpose. It is natural that in such cases the results would also not be in our favour.

Hence, pinpointing the purpose in our lives from time to time is a necessity for success and development. It is also obvious that the purpose in our lives should be aligned with our interests and likings failing which we might not enjoy working in those terrains.

When the purpose is well defined and in place then it acts as a great source of encouragement and motivates us to do our efforts in the desired direction of achieving our goals.

We all have some objectives and goals in our lives and we strive hard to attain them through hard work and concentrated efforts. That is what is called living for a purpose.

Purpose is the biggest motivational force that encourages us to work hard and achieve our objectives. People who always keep the purpose of their lives in their minds as a foremost entity generally get success in their endeavours.

The essence of all this is that a purpose is necessary in our lives and without that we cannot expect success and prosperity.

Discovering Purpose of Life

When I was a child my parents told me that my purpose of life was to study and score high.

I did not understand that at that time, I thought it was something to do with engaging my time and feeling high.

When I grew up then my parents told me and emphasized that my purpose of life was to secure a job and make a career.

I was also told by my relatives and friends that if I did that then only my life would become happier and merrier.

So far so good and I felt elated as I had academic degrees and I was sure that I would get the job of my choice.

But the reality was far behind from my thoughts and continuously struggling in the crowd of job seekers, I literally lost my voice.

My parents, relatives and friends advised me to acquire some skills and maybe to start some self -employed work in the neighbourhood.

This was a shock to me as I had no experience in any area or field where I could deliver services or sell goods or supply food.

Those difficult periods made me realize that probably I could not identify my purpose in life in time and was simply doing what was told.

I felt a strong need to identify what was my liking and interest and then concentrate in that area and try to find a livelihood in that fold.

That is how I could understand the importance of interest and liking in our lives and then identify our purpose within that boundary.

My academic qualifications remained in the background as they were and I started earning my livelihood by doing my choice of jobs though appearing to others as ordinary.

8. Eternal Learning Door

"Live as if you were to die tomorrow. Learn as if you were to
live forever."
-- Mahatma Gandhi

Pursuit for learning and acquiring knowledge is a continuous process in our lives. Some people have a strong desire for learning and it is apparent in their behaviour while in some it might be there in latent state not presenting it to outside world. Learning is the only thing which continuously changes our perspective of the world around us. It is not only the academic learning but learning in worldly matters, that is also something which equally matters.

Knowledge is generally compared with the vastness of the oceans and one can take as much learning from it as possible. The ocean of knowledge is a perpetual source of learning and enlightenment. One can have it as much as possible. There is no restraint whatsoever. It is only as how much can absorb and assimilate.

The interesting thing about learning is that more we learn more we find that we do not know much. So, there would always be a relentless pursuit to acquire more and more knowledge.

These ponderings about learning are presented in this short poem.

Eternal Learning Door

Relentless pursuit,
For learning and more learning.
Endless efforts,
For acquiring and creating.
A wealth of knowledge,
Emanating through silhouettes.
There is no end,
To the learning acrobats.
The learning desires,
Galloping in the mind.
They are but not,
The worldly kinds.
The honest pursuit,
Asking for more and more.
I am still searching,
The eternal learning door.

9. The Mighty Clouds

"Clouds in the sky very much resembles the thoughts in our minds! Both changes perpetually from one second to another!"
-- Mehmet Murat Ildan

Cloud formation had always charmed the people and evoked their sentiments since the time immortal and many poets and writers had described the beauty and magnificence of these floating and hovering bodies in the sky over our heads. They are so unique and widespread that they compel us to take note of them and of their manifestations in the sky.

Scientifically speaking, the Sun rays evaporate the water from the oceans which moves up in the atmosphere and forms clouds. These clouds then move as per the direction of the wind to other faraway places on the globe and then start precipitating in a favourable geographical location. So nature provides water to the landmasses on the Earth through this water cycle from oceans to clouds and then to land and back to the oceans. These mysterious vicious natural cycles sustain the life and vegetation on mother Earth. So, clouds are very important for human survival on the planet Earth. We must respect them from that point of view also.

A change from a sunny day to a cloudy day brings a lot of change in the moods of people and their behaviour is also affected accordingly. Some of the people feel good and rejoice in the formation of clouds in the sky while some others feel sad and even depressed with the semi darkness created by them. Clouds are the same but it is the perception of the person that matters who is observing them with a particular mindset.

In this composition, in addition to the main poem, I have tried to write an acrostic poem and also a haiku one on clouds depicting my understanding of them.

The mighty clouds

Clouds buildup after the scorching heat,
To provide water to us and cool us down.
The perennial source of life on earth,
They are coloured in white, black, and brown.
Clouds floating in the sky,
Like the cotton flakes abound.
When they accumulate and become dense,
Then they also make a thundering sound.
Clouds invoke soft emotions in us,
They bring pure motivations in us.
Clouds are a source of continuous joy,
They are actually nature's frequent toy.
The water oozing out of the clouds,
Is the pure heavenly nectar.
Which is for the human lives,
A most useful and important factor.
Sometimes clouds bring fear and despair,
Punishing humanity for its blunders.

Then they become a bit offending,

Bringing hurricanes here and there.

Remember, every cloud has a silver lining,

Though it could bring temporary sadness and grief.

But the respite will be soon available,

In the form of the next Sunshine brief.

Clouds - An Acrostic poem

Covering the sky above,

Lasting for days.

On the anvil they are,

Under the heavenly ways.

Doing their work persistently,

Sometimes they pass a few Sun rays.

Clouds - A haiku

Clouds are majestic,

They are the crowns under the sky,

Alas, they dissolve on earth.

10. Let Us Bury Our Secrets

"Secrets, silent, stony sit in the dark palaces of both our hearts: secrets weary of their tyranny: tyrants willing to be dethroned."
-- James Joyce

Most of the people in this world are keeping some secrets deep in their hearts. It could be anything of any nature like personal, financial, social, political, or related to physical disability.

It is difficult to explain the reasons as to why people keep secrets in their hearts but there could be different reasons for doing that varying from Individual to Individual.

Actually, when someone is hiding something from others, it means he has some apprehensions about it and he thinks that it should not come out in open publicly. In many cases, it is related to some personal ego or personal information or in extreme cases, it could also be some drug abuse or past criminal activity.

Though having secrets is very common in human beings but it has a darker side also. Many times, people suffer because of hiding some secrets deep in their hearts and always worrying as if what will happen if someone comes to know about them. Living in such continuous fear, stress, and tension in one's mind is not a good thing. If it is so then it will always be better to bury those secrets and forget about them. Sometimes, it may look a bit surprising thing, but even disclosing them to other people doesn't bring any harm or any bad situation to the keeper of that secret. In many cases, the person keeping the secrets might be having wrong apprehensions about the whole thing.

This set of two poems including one acrostic poem is an effort to bring all the above pondering and thinking about the secrets and ways to get rid of them. Why keep unnecessary tensions and stresses in our minds when we can very well live without them happily and joyfully.

Let us bury our secrets

Secrets are inevitable,

And are parts of our lives.

They are there since childhood,

Like the soul in our body thrives.

It is difficult to understand,

The psychology of secrets.

Why we have them and,

Keep them in deep pockets.

Children have secrets,

Of innocent nature.

But when they become adults,

Their secrets also turn mature.

Everyone will have some secrets,

Keeping them in a mysterious cage.

But when they are unearthed,

They could be a matter of disgrace.
Why can't we live in this world,
Just like an open book.
Where there on no secrets,
And no stories to cook.
We must nip in the bud,
The secrets in the forming.
That would make us trouble free,
When we get up every morning.
Let us bury the secrets,
In the deepest place around.
So that we don't get from it,
Even a whispering sound.

Secrets - An acrostic poem
Shame of mistakes done,
Easily generates secrets.
Caring to hide them,
Retains them to inlets.
Experiencing the pain,
Torture and continuous stress,
Slowly what the person gets.

11. Freedom from the Hot Prison

"Rain is grace; rain is the sky descending to the earth; without rain, there would be no life."
-- John Updike

This poem, coined by me, is the depiction of the change in weather from summer to rain in the Southeast part of Asian continent where people wait for rains at the end of every summer season and the onslaught of rains is a great sight and relief that cannot be described in words but can be felt only by the individuals.

In the South East Asian countries, the summer is quite intense and everyone looks for onslaught of rains and rainy season. Every year this yearning is there and all the living beings come out of their closet on arrival of rains.

The welcome to the rains is a spectacular scene when people rejoice and enjoy life in the outdoors even drenching in the rains and moving here and there singing songs of happiness and contentment.

As I am living in this part of globe, I also, like others, welcome and enjoy the onslaught of rains which bring not only a cool breeze but also bring a great respite from the summer which is now being forced by the rains to depart and remove its fangs over us. We all know that rains will be there for at least 2-3 months and the post rain autumn season will bring the beautiful and adorable autumn season which will be preceding the cool winters.

Freedom from the hot prison

The end of scorching summer,
Kick starts the rainy season.
People start feeling that,
They will get freedom from the hot prison.
The clouds are forming,
In a predetermined way.
Making a white canopy,
Obstructing the last Sun ray.
The heavy downpour starts,
With intermittent silence and thunder.
Taking away the heat of the earth,
The nature's magnificent wonder.
Slices of clouds one over other,
Slowly dissolving in snow and water.
People coming out and drenching in rain.
Loss of heavens is earthling's gain.
Birds coming out and fluttering their wings.
Flying when it is drizzling and doing their things.
Earth gets wet when the heavens please.
Earth understands that it is heaven's bleed.
Dry seeds present here and there,
And buried in ground.
Get excited and drink rain,

And swell to bigger size.
Soon they start producing roots,
And begin their upward journey.
To become saplings which would live,
To become tomorrow's greenery.
Rains have met the aspirations of the people,
The job is over and it will retreat soon.
The end of season is approaching near,
We will meet next year, good bye rain my dear.

12. I Can't Forget Her

"Loved you yesterday, love you still, always have, always will."
-- Elaine Davis

During our childhood we play with other children and enjoy the life in its best form. There was no responsibility, there was no worry of any kind, and there was no hassle of any sort at that time. Who will not long to go back to that type of life if given a chance?

Then we enter the age of adolescence which has its own charm. Getting young is like the opening of the bud to become a flower. That is the time when we meet others in a different perspective and feelings of love and infatuations start building between the people who were so far only the childhood friends. At that phase of our lives, we are introduced to an entirely new world of lust, desire, and possessiveness. Of course, it is natural to grow in that fashion and that is a truth of our lives. It is the way of nature and need of human bodies.

During such times many people get intimate with each other and promise to each other to be lifetime partners and take vow that they would remain in love for eternity.

But, alas, only a part of this story is true. The steaming relations come down calmly and become a thing of past and I think they are forgotten completely more quickly than they were acquired. It is not necessary that both the partners would be happy after that separation. It depends as who had been bitten more by the love bug.

This poem is an effort to depict the emotions and feelings of a person who is still remembering the sweet togetherness of the particular friend during the adolescent age.

I can't forget her

Childhood memories are a pleasant treasure,
The game we played with those risky adventures.
Some memories fade away some remain in our mind,
Our mind yearns and urges to go back to life of that kind.
The stage of adolescence brings new dimensions in our lives,
We are even introduced to love at first sights.
There are so many memories of those ecstatic situations,
Bringing us feelings of longing, love, and aspirations.
It finally happened called love at first sight,
There was no discussion there was no fight.
She came forward to fully meet my expectations,
Drowning me with all her magnificent affections.
Then one day the whole satire changed,
When she told me that it was the infatuation that prevailed.
She left for her own way and I felt deserted,
The love bite was very deep and it could not be rejected.
I reminded her to come back but she refused all the times,
She told me flatly that they were the childhood chimes.
She may be happy and contended in her own world,
I am still feeling infatuated with the old bird.

Love and then desert what is this human nature,
My problem and grief is that I can't forget her.

13. Good Health – A Wishful Thinking

"It is health that is the real wealth, and not pieces of gold and silver."

-- Mahatma Gandhi

There is an old saying that health is wealth. It still holds good and is true in its entirety. There are many schools of thoughts and doctrines which exist in this world for guiding people as how to keep a good health. Still, it is not known how effective they are and what is the authenticity of these sermons made by qualified doctors, health consultants, experienced people, seniors, and sometime the influential people.

Traditionally, people had tried various combination of herbs and natural products, medicines, exercises, different lifestyles, etc for keeping a good health but all those remedies are not successful in all the cases. Some of them might have a limited effect while some others may have no effect. Each and every approach for curing a person from ailments has certain limitations and their effectiveness is also not known with certainty whether it will be successful in a particular case or not. Medical science has done phenomenal progress in the area of curing diseases and ailments but still there are many grey areas and medical science has to find out new methods and new techniques for treating and eradicating all the ailments from human lives.

A good lifestyle coupled with a regime of regular exercises is said to be the main guiding factor for keeping a good health but that also has its own shortcomings as no one knows exact proportion of these things which one requires to undertake and the exact amount of consumption of food that is to be done. It is said that people should consume food as per their activity level. But no one goes for such precision in real life situations.

So, getting rid of diseases and ailments is as challenging today as it was in earlier times and we do not know how these things will be taken up in the coming times when we will have threat of more and more pollution and other chemical and biological threats in our environment and surroundings. Future could be more dreadful from this point of view.

This poem is written with these thoughts going in the background of my mind while the humans yearn for a happy and disease-free life and pray for it to the Almighty and try all sort of remedies available in this world.

Lately people are becoming more aware about Yoga, healthy food, and light exercises for keeping a good health and in coming times that would become a major factor towards which many of us would look for attaining better health.

Good health - A wishful thinking

Some are born healthy,

While some are born with ailments.

Some are very strong and robust,

While some have no healthy moments.
Nature is very much kind,
Providing air, water, and fire to all.
It gives enough food to us,
And water from the water falls.

Every particle in nature is,
Full of vigor and energy.
But same thing in some people,
Is creating a chronic allergy.
Physician say it is lack of immune,
While saints say it is fate.
Some people attribute it to skeleton bodies,
While others attribute it to high weight.
Scientists and scholars are relentlessly pursuing,
To unravel the mysteries of good health.
It is really very strange that,
We can't buy good health even with immense wealth.
Good health is a great ambition,
That many people dream.
But who cares in this world,
For the ailing person's scream.

I only wish that medical science,
Would soon resolve the good health mystery.
And with that the ailments and bad health,
Would be a thing of history.

14. I Do Not Fear

"Nothing in life is to be feared, it is only to be understood. Now is the time to understand more, so that we may fear less."
-- Marie Curie

Fear is a very common word but some people will have a feeling of insecurity and shivering if they hear this word or come across this feeling seriously. This word gets more effects in some situations, especially in isolated and dark areas. Fear is something that is inculcated in us right from our childhood and put in us by our parents and society during our growing up period. It is said that fear is a natural response to certain external conditions which are invoked by nature or some devilish elements which are said to be hovering in the space around us and seeing an opportune time they strike their pangs on us. It is also observed that some people are bold enough while some are very shaky and fear even the small things where there is nothing to fear. So, it is something that varies from individual to individual.

Some people view horror movies or horror shows and even read horror books and that also sometimes is a reason for conjecturing abnormal things in their lives when they are in a secluded and isolated place. Some scholars believe that fear is inside us and it is not in the surroundings. We only imagine its presence in the external world and our surroundings when actually it is sitting deep inside us only. Psychologists also agree with this viewpoint.

Still, many of us have fears in our minds and in our lives continuously and that are always hanging on our heads like a Damocles Sword.

Fear is not limited to nocturnal surroundings. It can be there in various forms and can manifest itself in myriads of ways. Some people fear their superiors, some fear the animals, some have fear of water bodies, while some fear of torrential rains, even there are people who fear their fellow humans which is, of course, a strange form of fearing but if it is there, it is there. It is said that there are some rare people who do not fear and are quite bold and do not believe in any supernatural powers. For them, the fear is only from natural disasters or man-made disasters. They are not afraid of anything probably because they are strong from their insides and have terrific confidence and willpower to face any adverse situation.

I do not fear

When I was a child,

I was told not to go out alone in the dark,

They took every sound as unusual though I knew it was a

dog's bark.

When I grew up my teachers told me not to go in bad

company,

I did not know what is a good or bad company,

As I couldn't afford that as I did not have any money.

When I grew up further and entered the adolescent age,

There was nothing to fear but the world was a difficult
relationship maze,
I wanted to make a career but in front of me, there was an
only haze.
So far there was nothing to fear and nothing to be afraid of,
As I had nothing in my hand to lose,
I was searching for a job with full intensity but getting
amused.
Finally, I got a job and settled in a career,
My colleagues told me that boss was a fearful person,
But contrary to the opinions I found him less offensive but
merrier.
My parents were very happy that I had a job and bad days
were gone,
They were insisting I marry and settle in family life,
And get rid of the fear of living alone.
But I was living fearlessly my own way,
Like a big bird wandering in the blue sky with its large
feathers,
People asked me haven't I been swept by the fears away.
I do not know what is this thing fear about which they are
talking,
I am still living in my own way,
And often go out in the dark nights for my usual walking.
I am still to face this entity which everyone calls fear,
If it comes in my way then I will have to find a way,
To make it my near and dear.

Fear - an acrostic poem

For those who never have fear of any kind,

Everything is normal and pleasant in life.

All are Godly and heavenly things for them,

Rare are such strong people in mankind.

15. Time Flows Forward

"Yesterday is gone. Tomorrow has not yet come. We have only today. Let us begin."
-- *Mother Theresa*

Time is the most mysterious entity in this universe. It flows in one direction only and that is the forward direction. The most interesting thing about time is that it neither stops nor it goes back. When time progresses ahead our age also increases and we grow up older and older. All other living beings also grow up with time. Some have a long life span while others have shorter life spans. Some small creatures live only for a few days. So, age of living beings is a relative thing.

Time does not wait for anyone and moves on relentlessly. It is obvious that different animals perceive time differently as per their life span. Human beings perceive time on the scale of 80-85 years which is the average life span of a person living on earth.The lives of heavenly bodies like stars in the sky are in millions of years till the source of light and energy is available in them. Till that time, they shine and illuminate their world around them like the Sun shining in our solar system. Incidentally, we all know that life is possible on earth because of sun rays and its warmth available to humans regularly year after year.

Measurement of time is also based on natural processes. For example, when Earth rotates around its axis and completes one rotation then it is called one day and that is why we see a new sunrise every morning. The interesting thing is that every day is a new day and every day gone is the past day, a part of history. The coming day in future is hidden from our sight and we do not know about that as what incidents will happen during that and what will be our activities in the future. We simply wait for it to come and embrace us in its boundaries. Further, one revolution of the Earth around the sun is equal to one year. The earth comes back to its original position after travelling around the Sun into such a great path experiencing different weathers on the way. By that time, we also grow up by one more year and our age is increased accordingly. Everything is related to this progress of time in forward direction only and this poem is an effort to showcase those peculiar characteristics and nature of time.

Time flows forward

Elapsed time does not come back,
Like the water flowing down a river.
It is like the help and charity,
Bestowed by a capable kind giver.
What we do today is fully engraved,
In the pages of the history sack.
Whatever we could not achieve in time,
Would form the accumulation we lack.
What we did in past cannot be modified,

As they are like the time rings in a tree.
Only when we complete our work today,
We would be contented, happy and free.
Time is the essence of everything, use it,
It is like the perpetual energy of the Sun.
The rays which came to us yesterday,
We had used it fully there and done.
I could have possibly done it earlier,
Or I would better do it sometime later.
These are the aberrated versions of,
All our useless false worldly matter.
Can I ever go back in the time,
Or can I stop it moving forward.
These questions often elude me much,
Answers to which are definitely very hard.

16. Photographs in My Album

"What I like about photographs is that they capture a moment that's gone forever, impossible to reproduce."
-- Karl Lagerfeld

This poem is inspired by the world 'photograph' and motivated me to recollect my old photographs that had been collected over a long time and had been placed in albums making a stack of them in my cupboard.

In old age, it is really very interesting and amusing to go through the personal photographs from childhood to the present consisting of so many occasions and gatherings with friends and relatives and locations where one had visited and functions and special occasions one had attended. The happenings during the last so many decades are just placed in front of us and showcase the most unforgettable moments in our lives which can now only be seen and recollected just in those photographs.

Starting from the black and white era of photography and ending with the latest digital high pixel photography, the collection contains all the hues from white to grey and grey to other vibrant colours. These old collections look like the shades of life during the past period that has been availed by oneself in one's life and all the milestones and main incidents seemed to be engraved in those physical records.

One interesting thing that has been seen in this context is that there is a hiatus in that collection as nowadays there are no physical prints for quite some time and every photograph taken after that hiatus is available either on the mobile or computer or a hard disk. So, there is an abrupt discontinuity, very much perceptible in that stack of albums as the later things are missing there.

This poem tries to depict the feeling of an old person who is almost at the last phase of his life and just going through the collection of photographs in the albums that are kept in the cupboard.

Photographs in my album

I was growing older and older,
Was at the fag end of my life.
I was happy and contented,
Did not have any conflict or strife.
My movements were restricted,
Confined to the house boundaries.
Only these four walls knew,
My deficiencies and my miseries.
And then one day when,
I happened to open my old cupboard.
I glanced upon the dusted albums,
Stacked aside and lying ignored.
I pulled them one by one,
And kept on a nearby table.

They were appearing to me,
As books containing some old fable.
Opening them one by one,
I travelled back in time.
My mind was resonating,
With that old charm of mine.
The old ones were black and white,
The later ones were fully coloured.
Some of them looked very familiar,
While others seemed to be blurred.
Small-medium and big sized,
Collection of the photograph.
They were covering me and my family,
Through the long chronograph.
My long life is just packed,
In these few album pages.
I am old but my mind is young,
For that life it still crazes.
I would be departing the world soon,
Leaving the album stack behind.
Those who want to meet me,
Can scan the albums and rewind.

17. Academic vs Skills

"Education is what remains after one has forgotten what one has learnt in school."
-- Albert Einstein

There are many developing or underdeveloped countries in this world, especially those which are having a large population and they are facing the problem of unemployment, poverty, and hunger. The education system in most of these places is old fashioned and limited to the academic acquisition of knowledge. The students generally do not get exposure to skill-based knowledge or job-oriented training. In such cases, they have a big problem of getting employment because good job positions are taken by the top-level performing students and the lower jobs are taken by the technical hands or skill-based people.

An ordinary student having passed his academic courses finds the world full of challenges and doesn't get success in getting a good job in spite of his high academic qualifications. This badly hurts one and then one thinks why one should not had gone for some technical and skill-based training in the first place itself instead of pursuing the default academic courses.

It is always a point of confusion for the guardians or the students to decide as to which line they should choose - pure academics or technical training. It is obvious that only the students having inclination, interest, and liking for the pure academic courses should pursue it so that they can go for higher education and possibly undertake research in their core areas and make a career in pure research or teaching or some career line like that. For the rest of the common students, it would be prudent to go for some job-oriented skill-based training which can provide them with a livelihood and source of sustained earnings.

This poem is the outcome and reflection of all those thoughts and the problems faced by so many young people across the globe.

Academic vs skills

I had studied in good Schools,
Which were capable of separating horses from the mules.
I was happy with my attainments,
hoping for a good career and achievements.
I had qualifications and hope in my veins,
But I was not aware of career making pains.
Applying for good positions here and there,
Trying to find out the luck in my share.
Everyone appreciated my knowledge,
But cut a sorry figure alike.
They wanted a skill-based person,
Not a Tom, Jerry, and Mike.
I realised the fallacy of my academics,
Not able to start a career.
I did not know any skilful job,

And that was the main barrier.
Someone advised me to do a short course,
And acquire some skills in hand.
Maybe I will not get a big job,
But it would place me in a mediocre band.
I was pondering on my destiny,
Searching for the answer in my mind.
When I had to be only skilful,
Then why do I have an education of that kind.
Pure academics is not for everyone,
Which is actually meant for researchers.
It is better to acquire some skills,
And go for self-employment strictures.

18. Humans Created Religion

"God has no religion."
-- Mahatma Gandhi

Most of the people believe that humans were created by God. At the same time, some believe that life on Earth was created by some biochemical reactions in nature under a conducive and suitable environment.

Whatever it is, with the advent of time as the human population increased across the globe societies started to distinguish themselves from each other in respect of their cultures, traditions, and religions. Different groups were following different religions and worshipping their respective Gods.

Subsequently, because of the fight for land and resources, wars and confrontations took place between various communities, countries, groups, or kingdoms. Kings, politicians, and leaders took advantage of their religion in these conflicts and told to their people that they were fighting for their religion to survive and sustain their growth on this planet. Common people took it very seriously and offered their services to fight the enemy in the name of religion.

This trend continued and even its intensity increased with time. Today politics and religion are intermingled to great extent and it is difficult to distinguish characteristics between them.

I have composed the following poem based on the above thoughts percolating in my mind.

Humans created religion

God created humans long back,

And placed them on earth.

He gave them a body and brain,

For living a life worth.

We used our brains,

But in spurious ways.

Whether a saint,

Or even a sage.

What we did,

Was unforgettable.

What we created,

Was unforgivable.

We created religion,

Not one but many.

Which created conflicts,

Rude, shrewd and uncanny.

We perceived different Gods,

To make our prominence.

We crafted different cultures,

No reason, no sense.

Cultures will never match,

And eventually will fight.

Humanity will doom,
And have its own plight.

19. Good Times are Like Rainbows

"It takes sunshine and rain to make a rainbow. There would be no rainbows without sunshine and rain."

-- Roy T. Bennett

We all know and well understand that life is an arduous journey full of challenges and problems. But we have to face them, we have to solve them, we have to conquer upon them, and then tread ahead through that difficult path.

During this journey, it is also possible that sometimes things happen in favourable ways and good times are also encountered which we all of course enjoy, relish, and feel good about it.

I have compared the good times in our lives with the rainbows that appear from time to time depending upon the direction of sunlight and the presence of small water droplets in the atmosphere. Rainbows are so colourful and bring a great feeling of rejoicing in our minds and from child to the elderly everyone enjoys that great beauty presented by the nature.

Good times in our lives are like the rainbows which suddenly come across our view and enthral us. They do not remain there for long and fade out soon but they again come back after a gap and again make our lives happy and pleasant. Let us hope and wish they come into our lives often.

Good times are like rainbows

The strange journey of life is,
Long, tedious, and difficult.
For treading ahead properly in it,
Everything is to be carefully dealt.
Every moment there are challenges,
Every moment there are problems.
We solve them one by one,
But many are emerging from sumps.
Occasionally we get help also,
From a kind hearted samaritan.
And also get help from a good friend,
Who saves us from the clutches of Satan.
When occasional good times come,
Everything becomes favourable and convenient.
But it is for a very short term,
As the new bigger challenges become pertinent.

20. A Thin Film in Between

"Our health is something we often take for granted. But there are some things in life that should never be taken for granted. Take care of yourself."

-- Catherine Pulsifer

There is an old saying - health is wealth. The essence of this saying is that we can enjoy life only when our health is in good condition and our body is in a good shape. A healthy person can work, play, travel, track, hike, swim, and carry out many other myriad activities in one's life. Without good health, all the avenues for activities are closed for us. We can only watch them happening but we can't participate in them. That is a miserable situation but the questions that come to our minds are - Is health in our hands? Can we maintain our health by resorting to a good lifestyle? These questions arise because we often observe that even a very healthy person suddenly gets ill and in no time is changed into a heap of blood and flesh. Why does it happen? What is his fault? What mistakes he committed?

Sometimes the transition from a good health situation to a bad one takes place so rapidly that one knows it only when one falls seriously ill. Then many of us start analysing where we went wrong in our routine and whether did some mistake of like say going out in a cold or hot or polluted environment. We can always find an approximate reason for falling ill but the fact is that it could be a wrong deduction many times because the actual reason is not understood in the majority of cases. Even the speculations and deductions of the best doctors fail in these matters.

There are no magic potions or magic tricks for making one's life healthy and at the most one can simply resort to a good lifestyle and consume healthy foods along with a routine of exercises and hope that it would keep one fit and healthy. Still, there are many things yet to understand and we must realize that there is a thin membrane between good and bad health and we do not know when that would break away. There are unknown and unseen forces in the nature which can break it at any opportune time.

This poem is a reflection of all these thoughts and though the subject is quite difficult and beyond the realm of materialistic thinking, I have tried to present it through this poem in the most simple and understandable language possible.

A thin film in between

Some people have good health,

while some do not have.

Reasons are unknown,

some say we are destiny's slave.

Heredity is one factor,

bringing up is another.

But still, there are differences,

Which are to be probed further.
A person born healthy,
May remain healthy till his death.
While a child born diseased,
struggles for minimal breath.
A rich person is not able to buy,
Good health with all the money.
While the poor are enjoying it,
With all their ways funny.
Good health might be,
A matter of good luck and chance.
Still, most of us try to maintain it,
Through our lifestyle plans.
Good health and bad health,
Are sitting near to each other.
There is a thin membrane between them,
Ready to break and flutter.
One can only wish,
To keep one's health in a good way.
Rest is not in our hands,
As it is destiny's play.

21. Happiness Lies Within

Happiness is an elusive entity for most of us and generally, we go on pursuing it relentlessly and searching for it in all the wrong places. It is the irony of our lives that most of the time we fail in achieving it. Happiness is a continuous requirement in our lives but most of us do not know how to get it. Some of us try to achieve it through materialistic resources and materialistic success but that also doesn't help much. Materialistic pleasures never end up in happiness. Some try it by minimizing their needs but it also works partially though many people believe that minimal living is a good way to achieve calm and peace in our lives. Still, we all are searching relentlessly as to where happiness lies.

In Indian mythology, there has been a great emphasis on lifestyle and it is mentioned that following a particular way of life and reducing worldly desires and temptations, one can achieve satisfaction and happiness. Many people believe in the doctrine of achieving spiritual attainments which finally brings happiness in one's life. One has to adopt that technique and find out whether that methodology is successful in bringing happiness to life. Likewise, there are different methods mentioned in different cultures for attaining calm and composed life but one has to learn it by trial and error only. It requires patience while treading that path of learning. Happiness cannot be achieved just by having materialistic pleasures in one's life. It requires a certain mindset that can only be maintained through the spiritual route and reduction of attachment to materialistic things. The spiritual route doesn't mean to stop doing the work, it means to work but not have expectations of glorious results from it. That is the basic premise under which attempts to achieve happiness can be successful.

In this poem, I have tried to depict the dwelling place of happiness which is not outside but is somewhere deep in our hearts only. What is required is that we have to introspect ourselves and find it lying there. If we stop worrying about all the unnecessary things in our lives then it would be possible to look within and find real solace and calm which only brings happiness to a person. Incidentally in this particular poem, I have also tried to make the poetic rhythm just by using three words in each line no more no less. It is not a new thing but I have used it to design this poem.

Happiness lies within

Searching for happiness,

In material things.

Yearning for success,

In worldly strings.

That unending struggle,

Keeping the pace.
Day and night,
That hollow race.
Happiness eluded me,
Hide and seek.
I simply became,
Mad and freak.
I went ahead,
I came back.
I scouted everywhere,
I was sad.
The agony within,
Like an evil.
I found myself,
Caught by devil.
Then it stroked,
Like a flash.
I stopped worrying,
Pain was less.
I peeped within,
It was blinking.
In my heart,
Happiness was singing.

22. Something is Nothing

"I am the wisest man alive, for I know one thing, and that is that I know nothing."

-- Plato

Writing something on nothing seems to be a difficult task but after thinking about it I found that spiritually speaking we all came from a sea of nothingness and will be spending some time here on this planet Earth only to go back and dissolve in the nothingness again. That might look like a philosophical way of looking at things but that works nicely to explain and understand this situation.

The birth of the universe and the creation of various life forms on this planet compel us to think of some ways in which so much of the material and life forms came from nowhere and after completing their life span are vanishing from the scene one by one. So, nothing is related to something in some peculiar ways and maybe science in the coming times would be able to decipher all those puzzles of life and death of men and conversion of material as perceived by us on this planet.

The ancient scholars defined zero as the mathematical symbol for nothing and it explained the absence of anything where nothingness existed. One end of the spectrum of something is zero and another end is infinite. If zero is nothing then infinite is everything. Some scholars believe that the universe is infinite in its size. It could also be true that heavenly bodies are simply floating in that endless void space. The interesting thing is that if we remove the material from that space then though it is infinite in size it is nothing as it becomes a void space spreading infinitely in all directions but containing nothing. The more we think about it more difficult and confusing it becomes.

In science, we studied mass-energy relations and we were told that mass and energy are interchangeable though mass is something that we physically perceive but energy can only be felt in some form and cannot be observed in material form. So, we might think that there is nothing but it could be some form of energy present there but not perceived by us. We only come to know about it, when we feel it through our senses, like the warmth of the Sun, cool touch of ice, heat from the fire, and many more alike.

Something in nothing

Universe is a big vacuum,
Where heavenly bodies float as specks.
It is the very grand example,
Of something in the nothingness.
Nothing cannot be measured,
As it has no shape no mass.
It does not belong to any category,
It does not belong to any class.
Evolution of life,
On the planet Earth.

Is a miracle of sort,
A matter of proud worth.
It is said that,
Elements combined to form life here.
But the question remains,
How the soul was joined there.
Consciousness was evolved,
Subsequent to creation of the souls.
Body had to take that burden,
Humans started to ponder their roles.
Soul is the source of life,
Rest is all immaterial.
Strange are the relationships,
Between mind and material.
Body is only a dwelling place,
While soul is something.
When soul leaves the body,
What remains is nothing.
Nothingness is nothing,
But things emerge from there.
It is nothing but,
Things mature and end there.

23. Time is Eternal

"Time is what we want most but what we use worst."
-- William Penn

Time is a unique entity. It flows forward. Time gone in past is gone for ever. There is no way we can go back and relive it.

Science treats time as a dimension in which activities are happening and new situations are emerging. Because there are changes in everything and we perceive it that way, we feel that time is progressing ahead.

Time has a spiritual meaning also. We all are growing older and destined to die one day. Our lives and longevity are denoted in terms of time only.

The measurement of time is related to Earth's rotation about its axis and also to its motion around the Sun which respectively makes day, night, and year for us. We measure all times with that cosmic reference.

The present poem is based on the above thoughts and is an effort to present time within a poetic boundary.

Time is Eternal

Time flows in forward direction,

To meet itself in future.

It is a strange entity,

Growing up in the lap of nature.

Was there a time zero,

Scholars strive to find.
Or it was perpetually there,
Of the same kind.
Time is immortal,
Like an infinite chime.
The world can end,
But not the time.
We can't keep it,
It slips from our hands.
It is present everywhere,
Even in unchartered lands.
Time is the eternal truth,
It was from ab initio.
Speed of time is same,
It has no high or low.

24. Sky is Weeping

"That's why; he's worried about how his life is turning out, and he's lonely, and lonely people are the bitterest of them all"
-- Nick Hornby

Loss of a relationship is sometimes painful and tortuous, especially for the sentimental and emotional people. Relationship could be of any type but when it had given a good companionship and support then its loss is a matter of big grief to the individual. Some people are able to quickly forget the bitter experiences of life but there are many who are too emotional to ignore those things happened in their lives and are driven to a sad consequent.

This poem is based on such premises where separation of companion is intolerable, especially when there is no perceptible reason for that. A person enters a stage of heartbreak and dejection leading to grief and misery.

Sky is weeping

Sky is weeping,

I am alone.

Sun was shining,

But now gone.

Garden was empty,

Plants were dry.

I was feeling lonely,

Nothing but to cry.
Remembrances,
Pricking my mind.
Unbearable and tortuous,
Pains of this kind.
The past is always,
Haunting my mind.
How can I continue,
Life of this kind.
There was no fight,
There was no conflict.
There was no noise,
There was no rift.
My companion left,
Without blaming me.
I am still not out,
From that reality.
I was not told,
What my mistake was.
I was left alone,
In misery's paws.
I am struggling,
To find my fault.
My life has come,
To a destined halt.

25. Elusive Happiness

"Happiness comes from you. No one else can make you happy.
You make you happy."
-- Beyoncé

Happiness is said to be a state of mind. Everyone wants to be happy but it is not easy to remain happy all the time.

Happiness is also considered a positive frame of things that makes people feel good. Who will not like to be happy? Everyone tries for that but due to various circumstances and situations it is not possible to achieve a continuum of happiness in one's life.

Many people strive and work hard towards achieving happiness in their lives but for many the end result is not positive and they feel as wasted their lives in that struggle.

In this poem I have depicted the various stages of one's life searching for that elusive happiness.

Elusive Happiness

Happiness an elusive entity,
It is shying away from us.
We always chase it but,
It is running away from us.
During my childhood,
I enjoyed playing games.
I felt very happy,

Giving toys some names.
I disliked school classes,
I was not academic type.
But I was always advised,
Study for a happy life.
Reluctantly I acquired,
Some basic education.
How that was going to make me happy,
I had no notion.
I did some odd jobs,
Earning money and spend my life.
I enjoyed working,
But did not feel satisfied.
I made some friends,
Enjoyed their company.
But seeing their selfishness,
I felt unhappy.
My parents told me,
It was time to get married.
Raising a family was the,
Happiest thing to be carried.
I was much excited,
Another chance to be happy.
But finding a suitable bride,
Was an endeavour tricky.
The search continued,
We found a good-looking girl.

I got married with her,
Offered her Silver, Gold, and pearl.
Life seemed quite good,
As a surprise.
But clashes and differences,
Started to arise.
Demands, nagging, and expectations,
Started showing their toll.
I simply found that,
I was not happy at all.
Separation seemed inevitable,
The only course logical.
I wanted to be a free person,
Requiring no obstacle.
I became a lonely soul,
But still was not happy.
I was getting old,
And waited in destiny's fold.
I gave my whole life,
Searching the elusive happiness.
I was still not happy,
Wasted the life precious.

www.ingramcontent.com/pod-product-compliance
Lightning Source LLC
Chambersburg PA
CBHW031326130726
47988CB00007B/3002